Kid's Library of Space Exploration

# Space Telescopes

# Kid's Library of Space Exploration

# Kid's Library of Space Exploration

# Space Telescopes

### Christie Marlowe

VILLAGE EARTH PRESS

**Kid's Library of Space Exploration: Space Telescopes**

Village Earth Press
Vestal, New York 13850
www.villageearthpress.com

First Printing
9 8 7 6 5 4 3 2 1

Series ISBN (paperback): 978-1-62524-444-4
ISBN (paperback): 978-1-62524-403-1
ebook ISBN: 978-1-62524-038-5
Library of Congress Control Number: 2014931523

Author: Marlowe, Christie.

# Contents

# ONE

# Early Telescopes

To ancient people, the night sky must have seemed magical. The daytime sky gave them less to wonder or dream about. Besides birds and clouds, all they could see above their heads in the daytime was the sun. They could not look directly at the sun, so it was hard to study or understand.

But at night, the sky was filled with stars. The moon replaced the sun. Since the moon is not nearly as bright as the sun, they could look directly at it. This made it much easier to study. They could even see a "face" on the moon's surface, what we now call the man in the moon. Today, we know that the moon is actually much smaller than the sun. It only seems bigger because it is much closer to the Earth.

Ancient people thought that the sun *revolved* around the Earth. We now know that the Earth revolves around the sun. We know that the sun isn't very different from many of the

**Revolved** means circled around in space. Our moon revolves around the Earth in a circle.

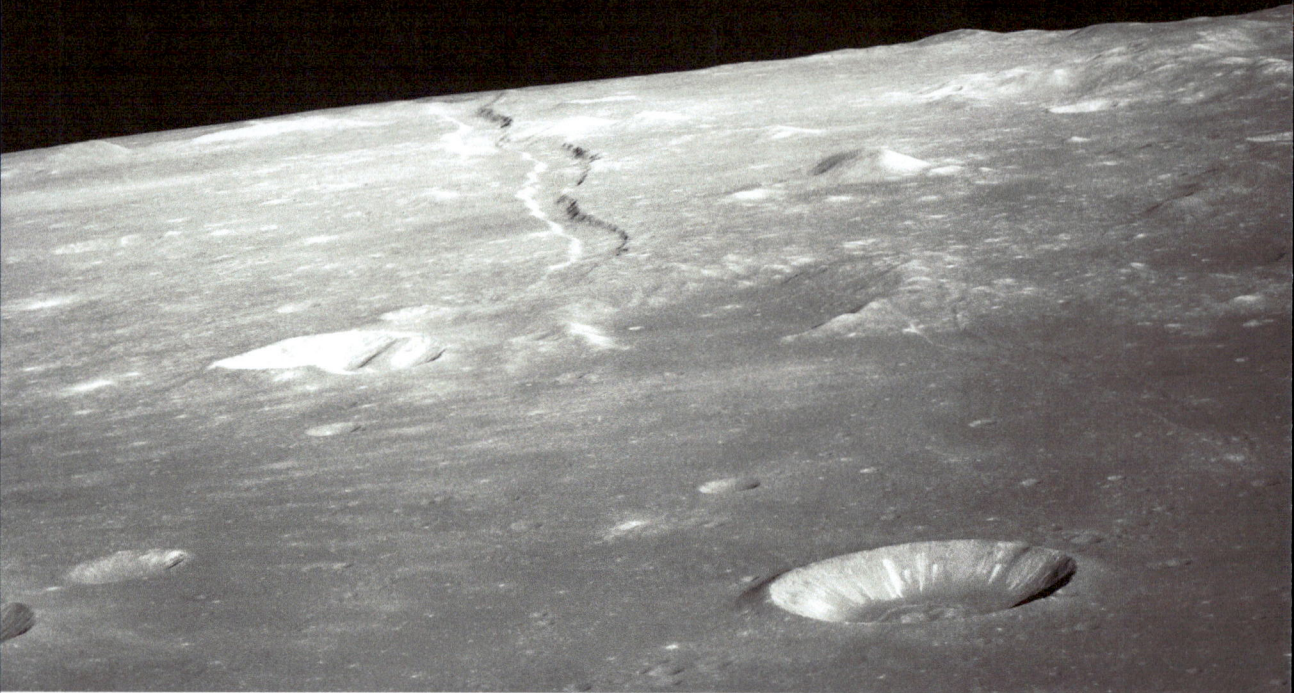

*The moon is the closest celestial object to us, and so ancient people must have thought about it a lot. Today, we know much more about it, and have even been there!*

stars in the sky. It is just closer. We even know now that many more stars burn in outer space than we can see when we look up into the night sky.

None of this knowledge would have been possible without the discovery of a tool that has helped us see much farther than our eyes ever could on their own. This tool is called the telescope.

## Our First Glimpses of the Stars

The history of the telescope involves many different tools that people used to look at objects. But the story begins with the first tool we had: our eyes!

Think of all the things you can see in the night sky. Most nights, for example, only part of the moon is visible. But on one night each month, the moon is full. And on another night, we are not able to see the moon at all. This is called the lunar *cycle*. Humans started keeping track of it over 25,000 years ago!

We now know that lunar cycles happen because the sun ever lights only one-half of the moon. Like the Earth, the moon's rotation causes day and night to move across its surface—but a lunar day is about twenty-eight Earth days! From Earth, we can see only the part of the moon that's lit. Depending on the Earth's position in relation to the moon, we may see a full circle (the

## Moon Goddess

The word "lunar" is used to refer to anything that has to do with the moon. It comes from the name of the Roman goddess of the moon, Luna.

half of the moon that's lit by the sun), or we may only see a fraction of that circle. When the dark side of the moon is facing the Earth, we cannot see the moon at all! This is called a "new moon."

Thousands of years ago, people didn't understand what caused the changes they saw in the night sky. But they began noticing patterns, like the lunar cycle. These patterns could be named and recorded. Recording and studying these patterns was very useful. Early sailors, on board their ships, were able to tell where they were by studying the positions of the moon and the stars in the night sky. They used the patterns in the night sky for *navigation*.

Humans believed that studying celestial bodies—stars, the moon, and the sun—could teach them important things about the world. Astrologers were the people who studied these patterns.

Astrologers thought the movement of the stars could be used to *predict* when were the best times to hunt, fish, plant, harvest, marry, and fight. Today, people might look in the newspaper to read their astrological horoscope just for fun, but in ancient times, astrology was considered to be a very serious study. Rulers asked astrologers for their advice. Astrology shaped many human affairs.

Some people still study astrology today. Modern-day astrologists believe that the movement of the stars shapes

A **cycle** is a series of steps that repeats over and over again.

**Navigation** is figuring out where you are in the world and where you need to go.

When you **predict** something, you make a guess about what's going to happen in the future.

*Galileo is widely known as a pioneer of astronomy. He was the first to see many of the objects in the night sky, including the four largest moons of Jupiter, which are today named after him.*

our lives. But today, astrology is no longer considered a science. The science of astronomy has replaced the old astrological studies. The foundations of modern-day astronomy, however, were built on the ancient astrologers' work.

Early astrologers measured the positions and movements of the celestial bodies. They made very exact measurements. Based on these, they were able to figure out the size of the Earth, the moon, and the sun. These measurements even told them how far away the sun and the moon are from the Earth. They did all this using only their eyes to study the night sky!

# The Invention of the Telescope

## The Astrolabe

The telescope was not the first tool invented for studying celestial bodies. An ancient Greek astronomer named Hipparchus is usually given the credit for inventing the astrolabe (which means "star-taker") in 150 BCE. For hundreds of years, astronomers and navigators used this tool to take better measurements of the celestial bodies. It was a little like a very early computer. It allowed people to locate and predict the positions of the planets, stars, moon, and sun. It could also be used to determine time and latitude.

A German glasses maker named Hans Lippershey wrote the first plans for a working telescope. Some people think that Lippershey came up with the idea himself. Other people say that he stole the idea from someone else or from one of the men who worked for him. One story even goes that two children were playing with eyeglass lenses in Lippershey's shop. The children noticed that a far-away weathervane looked much closer if they looked at it through two lenses put together. No matter how Lippershey came up with the idea, his plan for a tool he called "For Seeing Things Far Away as if They Were Nearby" was the first recorded example of a working telescope.

Lippershey's plan was sent to many countries in Europe. His invention attracted the attention of many people, especially astronomers. Improvements were quickly made to Lippershey's basic plan. Only a few months later, the English astronomer Thomas Harriot used a more powerful telescope to draw the surface of the moon. Harriot's drawings

were the first time that anyone had recorded a celestial body by looking at it through a telescope!

The Italian scientist Galileo Galilee made more important improvements on the telescope. Galileo made some very important astronomical discoveries with his telescope. Some of those discoveries got him in trouble!

Up until Galileo's time, people thought that the moon's surface was completely smooth. They thought that the dark spots on the moon came from somewhere inside the sphere, like rotten spots inside an apple. Using the telescope, Galileo made very careful recordings of the moon. He discovered that the dark spots were actually shadows cast by large mountains on the moon. The moon's surface was uneven.

A few years earlier, a Polish astronomer named Nicolaus Copernicus had told the world that he believed the Earth went around the sun, instead of the other way around. Up until then, most people believed that the Earth was at the center of the universe. They believed that the sun, the planets, and the stars all revolved around the Earth. In a book published in 1543, Copernicus said that the opposite was true. He said that actually the Earth and the other planets revolved around the sun. Galileo used his telescope to examine the sky—and decided that Copernicus was right.

Many people did not like this idea. They thought that God had made the

## Twinkle, Twinkle, Little Star

We often say that stars "twinkle." They seem to grow brighter and dimmer very quickly. Stars' light doesn't actually change, though. In order for the light to reach us on Earth, it has to pass through our atmosphere. The Earth's atmosphere is often windy, and clouds come and go. This means that the stars' light is always passing through different thicknesses of atmosphere. These small changes are what make stars twinkle.

*Lyman Spitzer's idea to put telescopes outside of the Earth's atmosphere would prove to be a good one. Many space telescopes have been launched since then, including the Spitzer Space Telescope, named after him.*

universe for human beings. They thought that the ideas Galileo and Copernicus were teaching went against the Bible. The Christian church was very powerful in these days, and the leaders of the church were so upset that they banned Copernicus' ideas. Another astronomer, Giordano Bruno, was even burned at the stake for believing Copernicus!

But Galileo didn't let that stop him. In 1632, he published a book of evidence proving that Copernicus was right—the Earth did indeed revolve around the sun. Much of this evidence, Galileo had observed through his telescope.

People still did not want to believe this new idea. They did not want to change the way they thought about the world. Galileo was arrested and sent to court. In the end, he was sentenced to be imprisoned in his home for the rest of his life. The world refused to accept that he was right until after he had died.

## Electromagnetic Radiation

Electromagnetic radiation is energy that travels in waves. Light is one kind of electromagnetic radiation. Many different kinds of electromagnetic radiation also travel to Earth through space. Light is visible to our eyes, while other kinds aren't.

# Lyman Spitzer's Big Idea

Since the invention of the first telescopes, astronomers have had one goal in mind—they have always wanted to see farther and more clearly into outer space. Early telescopes helped them learn a lot. But these early telescopes were very limited. You couldn't use them to look into the sky during the day, when the light of the sun interfered. During the night, clouds, fog, and haze could get in the way of astronomers' vision.

The **atmosphere** is the layer of gases that surrounds the Earth. It gives us the oxygen we need to breathe and protects us from space.

And even on a clear night, the Earth's *atmosphere* still interferes with our ability to see the stars.

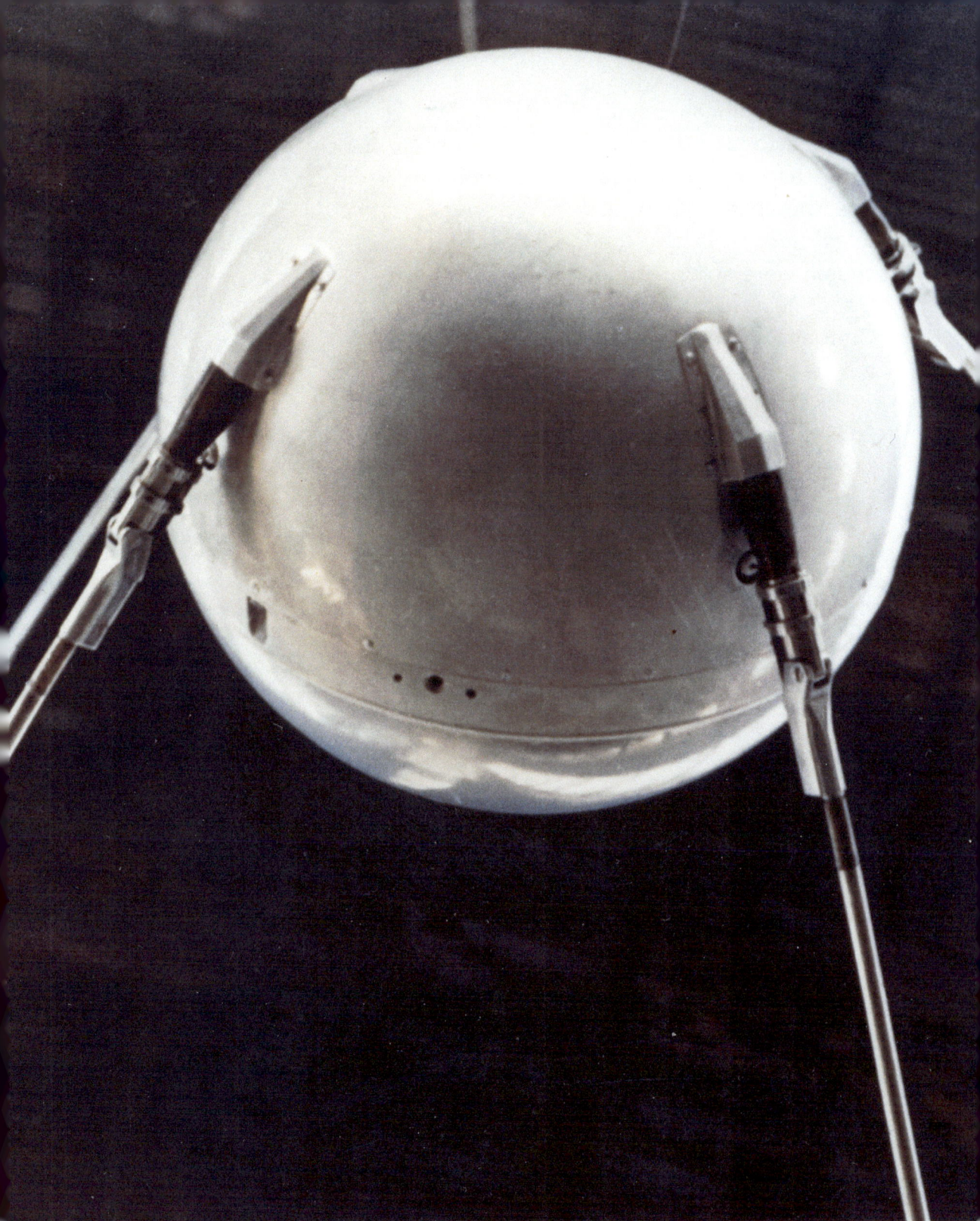

*Until* Sputnik 1, *no one was even sure that it was possible to put manmade objects into space.* Sputnik *couldn't do much, but it was an important step toward putting more advanced satellites into orbit.*

In 1923, a German named Hermann Oberth—who is considered to be one of the fathers of modern rocketships—published an article that mentioned how a telescope could be pushed into Earth's orbit by a rocket. Then, in 1946, an American astronomer named Lyman Spitzer did more work on this idea. He published a paper that claimed that sending a large telescope into outer space would solve many of astronomers' problems.

It was a very big idea. It was also a good idea—except how could people put a telescope in outer space? How could they get it there?

Ten years later, Russian scientists launched the first human-made satellite. A satellite is any object that circles around a planet or a star. The moon is the Earth's satellite because it revolves around our planet. And now human beings had proven that a human-made object could also be a satellite.

This first satellite, known as *Sputnik*, wasn't very big. It was only 28 inches (71 cm) long. It weighed about 183 pounds (83 kg). A space telescope would have to be much larger than that. Scientists still had more to learn before they could launch a space telescope into outer space. But they were on the right track. Lyman Spitzer's big idea no longer seemed impossible!

# Find Out Even More

Reading a book like the one you have in your hands is a great way to learn more about the things you're interested in. The author searched for information about space telescopes. She found interesting facts and put them together for you. But one book can never hold all the information about a subject as amazing as space telescopes. The author had to choose which facts to put in the book and which to leave out. To find out more about the Hubble telescope and other space telescopes, you'll have to read more than one book.

Finding other books about space telescopes is easy. Take a trip to your nearest library. You may have a library in your school or in your town. At the library, check out the card catalog and search for books on space telescopes. Your library might have a computer you can use to search for books. You can also ask the librarian for help finding books if you have trouble. Try looking for some of the books below about space, astronomy, and the Hubble telescope.

Carruthers, Margaret W. *The Hubble Space Telescope*. New York: Children's Press, 2004.

Dickinson, Terrance. *NightWatch: A Practical Guide to Viewing the Universe*. Richmond Hill, Ontario: Firefly Books, 2006.

Scott, Elaine. *Space, Stars, and the Beginning of Time: What the Hubble Telescope Saw*. New York:  Clarion Books, 2011.

Lippincott, Kristen. *Astronomy.* New York: DK Eyewitness Books, 2008.

Take a close look at one of the books you find in the library. In the front of the book, look at the table of contents. Does the book have a glossary (a list of the difficult words in the book) or index? Flip to one of the chapters in the book and look through it. Ask yourself a few questions after you've looked at the book for a while.

1.  How well do you understand the book? Finding a book that you can understand is a big part of becoming a better reader. Not every book is right for every person. You have to find a book that works for you. Does the book match your reading level? Is it too hard to read? Is it too easy? Don't forget to challenge yourself!
2.  How is the information in the book organized? Does the table of contents help you find information you're looking for? What about the index?
3.  Try using the table of contents or index to find information about space you didn't read in this book. Can you find new information easily?
4.  Does the book have pictures? Do they help you learn more about the subject? Seeing pictures or photos of the things you're reading about can be a fun way to learn more.
5.  Do you like the book? Do you want to read more?

# TWO

# The Hubble Telescope

In 1990, America's National Aeronautics and Space Administration (NASA) launched the Hubble Space Telescope into space. Lyman Spitzer's dream had become a reality!

The space telescope was a big project that took a lot of time and hard work. Lots of new *technology* made it possible. To this day, it is one of the most *advanced* telescopes humans have created. Years of *research* made it possible. Earlier space telescopes helped scientists understand the problems they needed to solve before the Hubble could be launched.

**Technology** is something humans invent to make something easier.

When something is **advanced**, it is the best technology that has been invented.

**Research** is studying to learn new things about science and create new inventions.

*Although the original OAO telescope failed after only three days, it was the first look astronomers had of distant objects without the Earth's atmosphere getting in the way. Using what they learned from OAO's failure, scientists were able to make OAO-2 and Hubble successful.*

# The First Space Telescopes

Back in 1962, NASA launched the Orbiting Solar Observatory (OSO). It was a kind of telescope. It didn't have a lens for magnifying light, though. Instead, its job was to pick up other kinds of radiation—ultraviolet, X-ray, and gamma-ray radiation. These kinds of electromagnetic radiation are not visible to the human eye. But scientists could still use them to learn more about space. The same year, an orbiting solar telescope was launched by the United Kingdom as part of the Ariel space program. Then in 1966, NASA launched the first Orbiting Astronomical Observatory (OAO) *mission*. The mission failed, though, because the observatory's battery quit after only three days. Two years later, NASA tried again and launched OAO-2. The observatory took ultraviolet readings of stars and galaxies. It was only expected to last a year, but this time the battery kept on working. It continued to send back messages to scientists on Earth until 1972.

# The Large Space Telescope

NASA gave Lyman Spitzer the job of leading a group of scientists to figure out what it would take to send a larger and more complicated telescope into space. Three years later, Spitzer's group published a report that explained how a large space telescope should be designed.

Their plan would take a lot of technology and a lot of money. They *estimated* that the project would cost between 400 and 500 million dollars! Many government leaders didn't think that this much money should be spent on a space telescope. But Lyman Spitzer and the other scientists didn't give up. Astronomers worked together to persuade the government that a space telescope would be worth the money it would take to build it and get it out into space.

Meanwhile, in 1969, NASA successfully sent a man to the

A **mission** is a trip taken to achieve a goal or to fulfil some purpose. For example, the OAO's mission was to study X-rays and gamma radiation in space.

**Estimated** means made a good guess, often based on past experience or similar situations.

## Edwin Hubble

Edwin Hubble was born in 1889 and died in 1953. During his lifetime, he made many important discoveries. His observations of stars and space seemed to show that our universe is expanding. He also identified other galaxies besides our Milky Way. These galaxies are so far away that astronomers had thought they were just clouds of dust. By showing that galaxies existed outside the Milky Way, Hubble proved that the universe is bigger than our own galaxy.

moon. The mission was such a success that NASA wanted to begin more projects. The American government agreed to set aside money to build a large space telescope.

In 1975 the European Space Agency and NASA began to work together on the Large Space Telescope. By 1979, astronauts were training for the mission.

When you move into *orbit* around the Earth, objects (including astronauts) seem weightless. To train for being in space to work on the Large Space Telescope, astronauts worked on a fake space telescope underwater. Being underwater feels a lot like being weightless.

Finally, in 1981, the Large Space Telescope was ready. But it couldn't be put together on Earth. A space shuttle would need to carry it into space where it would be built. It took another four more years to build the space shuttle.

The Large Space Telescope was renamed the Hubble Space Telescope in 1983. It was named after American astronomer Edwin Hubble.

## Tragedy

The Hubble Telescope was scheduled to launch into outer space in 1986. But a few months before the telescope's launch, the Space Shuttle *Challenger* exploded. The *Challenger* was carrying a schoolteacher named Christa McAuliffe. She would have been the first non-scientist in outer space. Christa and six other people died in the *Chal-*

**Orbit** means circle high above the surface. Spaceships need to move very fast to avoid falling back to Earth—when they're doing this, they're in orbit.

*When Hubble was first launched, the images that it sent back weren't as clear as scientists were hoping. By doing a spacewalk, or EVA, astronauts were able to fix the problem.*

*lenger* explosion. People were very upset. NASA stopped sending rockets into outer space for two years.

The Hubble Telescope was moved into storage. But scientists continued to work on the telescope. They made many small improvements to the telescope and the shuttle that would carry it into space.

## Success!

On April 24, 1990, the Hubble Telescope was finally launched into outer space. Many astronomers had been waiting patiently for this day. The Hubble Space Telescope began to send pictures back to Earth. But at

## Hubble's Instruments

There are many complex parts that make the HST work.

- The Wide Field Camera 3 is the main lens on the Hubble. It is able to take pictures of visible and near-visible light.
- The Cosmic Origins Spectrograph is another lens that sees ultraviolet light. Ultraviolet light is another form of electromagnetic radiation.
- The Advanced Camera for Surveys sees visible light and is designed to study some of the earliest activity in the universe.
- The Space Telescope Imaging Spectrograph sees multiple forms of electromagnetic radiation. It is mainly used to find black holes, regions of space with such dense gravity that even light can't escape from them.
- The Near Infrared Camera and Multi-Object Spectrometer sees infrared light, another form of electromagnetic radiation.
- Fine Guidance Sensors are devices that keep Hubble pointed in the right direction.

first there was a problem. The pictures were very blurry.

Scientists figured out what the problem was. The Hubble Telescope works because light enters the telescope and hits a large, curved mirror. The mirror reflects the light into another smaller mirror. The smaller mirror sends the light back through a small hole in the large mirror. This image then enters the equipment that sends the image back to Earth. The images were blurry because the large mirror was not curved enough. The mirror's flaw was very tiny. But it was just big enough to **distort** the images the Hubble was capturing with its lens.

The Hubble Telescope had been designed so that parts could be fixed and replaced in space. This tiny flaw was actually an opportunity. Scientists were excited to repair the Hubble. It gave them a new mission, a new chance to learn more about space.

Astronauts spent the next eleven months preparing for a very important job. These astronauts were about to perform one of the most **complex** space missions in history.

Late in 1993, the Space Shuttle *Endeavour* was launched to fix the problem. The repair took about a week. It went very well. Not only did astronauts fix the problem, but they also checked and replaced a number of other parts.

A few days later, the Hubble Space Telescope began sending sharp photographs back to Earth. The pictures were everything that Spitzer had promised back in 1947. For the first time, we were able to see clearly into outer space. The pictures were beautiful. And they could be used to find out more about our universe than anyone could imagine!

When you **distort** something, you warp or twist it.

**Complex** means complicated or difficult.

Four other service missions to the Hubble Space Telescope have taken place since then. On two of these missions, new parts were installed that made the Hubble even more powerful.

# Studying the Planets and Stars

The Hubble Telescope lets us see many things. Many of these objects can also be seen from high-powered telescopes located on Earth. But the Hubble Telescope allows us to see these objects in amazing detail!

The Hubble has been able to take many pictures of stars and planets being created. Stars form in large clouds of dust and gas that are pulled together by gravity. When enough dust and gas is pulled tightly together, the young stars erupt and spread leftover dust and electromagnetic radiation into space. Some of this dust gets pulled back into the star, which allows it to grow. Due to the gravity of the young star, the rest of the dust begins to revolve around it. Eventually, the dust collects together and forms planets.

Before the Hubble Telescope, astronomers had seen the birth of stars, but they had believed that viewing the dust that creates planets was impossible. They thought that interference from the young stars would get in the way. The Hubble Telescope proved them wrong. The pictures that the Hubble has taken of planets and stars being formed are teaching scientists a lot about the beginnings of the Earth, the sun, and our solar system.

The formation of stars and planets isn't all that the telescope sees. The Hubble has proven useful in studying planets beyond our solar system. Before the Hubble Telescope, the only way astronomers could study the planets that orbit other stars is by observing them when they passed in front of a star. When that happened, the planet would look like a tiny black sphere. The light from the star behind the planet, though, would make it hard for astronomers to see the planet clearly.

*The Hubble Space Telescope showed us parts of the universe that we had never seen before—but it was only the beginning of what we could learn from space telescopes!*

Now, scientists could even take the first measurements of the atmospheres of these distant planets. They did this by studying some of the electromagnetic radiation produced by the planets. They were even able to find the first organic molecules on distant planets. An organic molecule is any combination of chemicals that contains carbon. Carbon is an element that is contained in every living thing on Earth. Scientists were excited to discover the building blocks of life outside our solar system!

In 2008, the Hubble did something that no one had thought was possible. It took the first visible picture of one of these distant planets. This planet is called Fomalhaut b, and it is over 150 trillion miles away! Scientists are still not completely sure that the picture shows a planet. Some scientists worry that it is actually just a huge cloud of dust. It might also be a bunch of rubble. In 2012, though, new evidence came in showing that Fomalhaut b is actually a massive planet hidden inside a large cloud of dust.

# The History of the Universe

Light travels very quickly. It travels so quickly that it would be able to circle the Earth more than seven times in one second! But even though light travels so quickly, it still takes a long time to reach us when it has to travel billions and billions of miles across the universe. This means that by the time light reaches us from distant stars, it has been trav-

**Galaxies** are huge groups of millions or billions of stars, held together by gravity. The Milky Way that we live in is a galaxy.

eling for tens, thousands, or even billions of years. Looking at distant objects through the Hubble Telescope is very much like looking back in time. It's kind of a like a time machine!

Usually, when the Hubble takes a picture, it absorbs light for a few hours. Scientists decided to turn Hubble toward what looked like an empty patch of sky—and then they let the Hubble take in light for ten days. The Hubble Telescope won't operate forever, and scientists were afraid they were wasting a lot of the telescope's time. But the result of the experiment was amazing. The Hubble captured the light of more than 3,000 very old *galaxies*. These early galaxies were nothing like scientists expected. Some of them were very small and had strange shapes. Scientists got clues as to how our own galaxy may have grown too.

The Hubble has also helped solve one very important question—how old is the universe? Scientists before the Hubble Telescope had decided that the universe is between ten and twenty billion years old. But that's a pretty large age range! Scientists wanted a more exact answer.

Scientists believe that the universe began at the Big Bang, the moment when everything in the world started expanding out from a small, dense point where it began. Now astronomers used the Hubble to study the rate at which galaxies move away from each other. They examined the distances between galaxies. Using that information, scientists were able to determine that the universe is actually about 13.8 billion years old!

The Hubble Telescope has helped us learn more than we could have ever possibly dreamed. The night sky filled ancient people with wonder. But imagine what they would have thought if they had seen distant galaxies and the birth of stars and planets!

# Find Out Even More

Books only have so many pages. No book has enough space to cover everything about a subject. On the Internet, however, there is no limit. Online, millions of websites have thousands of words and pictures about every subject you can think of. The only problem is, you have to find all the facts yourself. There is no one author to help organize the information online. Instead, there are millions of authors organizing smaller bits of information. You have to go find the authors and information you want to read on the Internet.

Thankfully, search engines like Google or Bing are a good way to sort through all the information. Search engines find websites for you based on words you type into the search bar. Try searching for some of the key words below.

space telescopes
early astrologers
Hans Lippershey
Lyman Spitzer
astronomy
history of telescopes
Hubble space telescope
*Challenger*
NASA
European Space Agency

Google finds around 160,000,000 results when you search for NASA. You'll never be able to see every site about NASA. But there are a few important sites (like NASA's own website) that are good sources of information about the subject.

The Internet is an excellent way to learn more about many things, but it's not perfect.

Search engines like Google and Bing can only find sites based on what key words you use, so picking the right words is important. The wrong key words can get you results that aren't even close to what you're searching for.

# THREE

# Other Space Telescopes

The Hubble Telescope has been an important tool for studying the universe. But it is not the only telescope in the sky. In fact, the Hubble's uses are limited. It mostly sees visible light. In order to study the other forms of electromagnetic radiation, other space telescopes were needed.

## The Chandra X-Ray Observatory

Riccardo Giacconi and Harvey Tananbaum came up with an idea for a different kind of space telescope. They brought the ideas for the Chandra X-ray Observatory to NASA in 1976. Their plan was for a space telescope that would pick up X-rays and ultraviolet light from outer space.

These kinds of electromagnetic radiation are sent out from very hot regions of space. They can be dangerous to humans. Our sun also sends out X-rays and ultraviolet light, but our atmosphere absorbs most of it.

*Each space telescope can only "see" a small part of the light released by an object. This image of the M83 galaxy was made by combining infrared information from Spitzer, X-rays from Chandra, and visible light from Hubble.*

## Who Was Chandra?

The Chandra X-ray Observatory was named after a man named Subrahman-yan Chandrasekhar. Known to most people simply as Chandra, he came to the United States from India in 1937 and became an American citizen in 1953. He was one of the first scientists to combine physics and astronomy. Early in his career he showed that there is an upper limit—now called the Chandrasekhar Limit—to the mass of a white dwarf star. After millions of years, when a star like our sun uses up its fuel, it will eventually collapse and turn into a white dwarf star. Chandra proved that a white dwarf that is too big will either explode or form a black hole. In 1983, Chandra received the Nobel Prize for his work.

Chandra was a good name for this scientist—and it is a good name for the X-ray observatory too—because Chandra is also the name of a Hindu moon god. The god Chandra is described as being young and beautiful. Every night, he rides a chariot pulled by ten white horses across the sky. He is also called the Lord of the Night, the One Who Illuminates the Night, and the Bright Drop.

The atmosphere protects us from radiation that could harm us. Chandra would allow scientists to study these forms of radiation without putting themselves in danger.

While scientists worked to design Chandra, in the meantime, NASA launched the first imaging X-ray telescope, Einstein, in 1978. By 1979, the plans for Chandra were complete—but NASA wasn't ready to build it. Like the Hubble Space Telescope, Chandra would also be very expensive to build. The Hubble Space Telescope was already under construction, and each year, it cost even more money and time than anyone had expected. No one wanted to build another large telescope like Chandra until the Hubble was completed.

Work continued on the Chandra project through the 1980s and 1990s. In 1992, to reduce costs, the observatory was redesigned. Finally, in 1999 the Space Shuttle *Columbia* launched Chandra. At 22,753 kilograms (50,162 pounds), it was the heaviest load ever launched by a shuttle. Now the space observatory could finally get to work!

Like the Hubble Telescope, the Chandra X-ray Observatory is an incredible time machine. It studies parts of space that existed 10 billion

This supernova remnant in the constellation Cassiopeia is one of the objects Chandra has studied. Although it can barely be seen at all with the naked eye, this cloud of gas is more than 100 light years (588,000,000,000,000 miles) across!

*Instead of being launched from the ground in its own rocket, Chandra was launched in the cargo bay of the Space Shuttle* Columbia. *This allowed astronauts to make any last-second adjustments or repairs to the telescope, in case something went wrong.*

years ago. It observes X-rays from clouds of gas so enormous that it takes light more than five million years to go from one side to the other.

Some of the most important discoveries that Chandra has made have to do with black holes. A black hole is a region of space where the gravity is so great that nothing can escape from it, even light. This means that it is invisible. Scientists can tell it's there, though, because of the way things act around it. Although nothing can escape a black hole's huge gravity, the Chandra X-ray Observatory will be able to study particles up to the last millisecond before they are sucked inside. This information may help scientists understand black holes better.

*One of the most important discoveries made with infrared telescopes is the presence of water in the universe. The clouds in the center of this baby solar system contain enough water to fill the Earth's oceans five times over.*

# Infrared Telescopes

The Spitzer Space Telescope is named after Lyman Spitzer, who was the one who came up with the idea for putting telescopes in outer space. The Spitzer is designed to pick up infrared light. Like visible light and X-rays, infrared light is another form of electromagnetic radiation. We feel infrared light as heat.

In 1983, the United Kingdom, the Netherlands, and the United States worked together to launch into space an earlier and simpler version of the Spitzer Space Telescope, the Infrared Astronomical Satellite (IRAS). The IRAS needed to be kept very cold so that it could pick up small differences in heat (infrared radiation). It takes a lot of energy to keep something cold, though. The IRAS used a type of gas called helium to keep it cold.

The IRAS discovered several asteroids and comets. It also sent back information about the center of the Milky Way. After ten months, though, the IRAS ran out of helium. It stopped sending messages to scientists back on Earth.

But scientists were hungry for more. In 1995, the European Space Agency, with help from Japan and the United States, launched the Infrared Space Observatory (ISO). It sent messages back to the Earth until 1998—and then it too, like the IRAS, ran out of helium. Without helium, the ISO quickly became too hot to do its job.

While it was working, however, the ISO made important discoveries. It *detected* water *vapor* in the regions of space where stars form. It discovered planets being formed around old and dying stars. (Until then, astronomers had believed that planets only formed around young stars.) It found out what chemicals are in the atmospheres of some of the planets in our own solar system. And it studied stars being born.

Scientists knew that another infrared observatory could send them more important information. In 2003, NASA launched another infrared telescope, the Spitzer Space Telescope. This time they sent the telescope farther out into space, so that it orbited the sun far away from the Earth. This meant that the Earth's heat didn't reach it. It didn't need to use as much helium to stay cold, so it could keep working longer. It was able to send messages back to Earth until 2009.

Like the other space telescopes, the Spitzer made some very important discoveries. In 2005, the Spitzer was the first telescope to capture light from a planet outside our solar system. The Spitzer wasn't able to see the planet. But it was able to tell it was there.

**Detected** means to have found something.

**Vapor** is the gas form of something. When you boil a pot of water, it is turning into water vapor.

# Locations of Kepler Planet Candidates

*As of January 7, 2013*

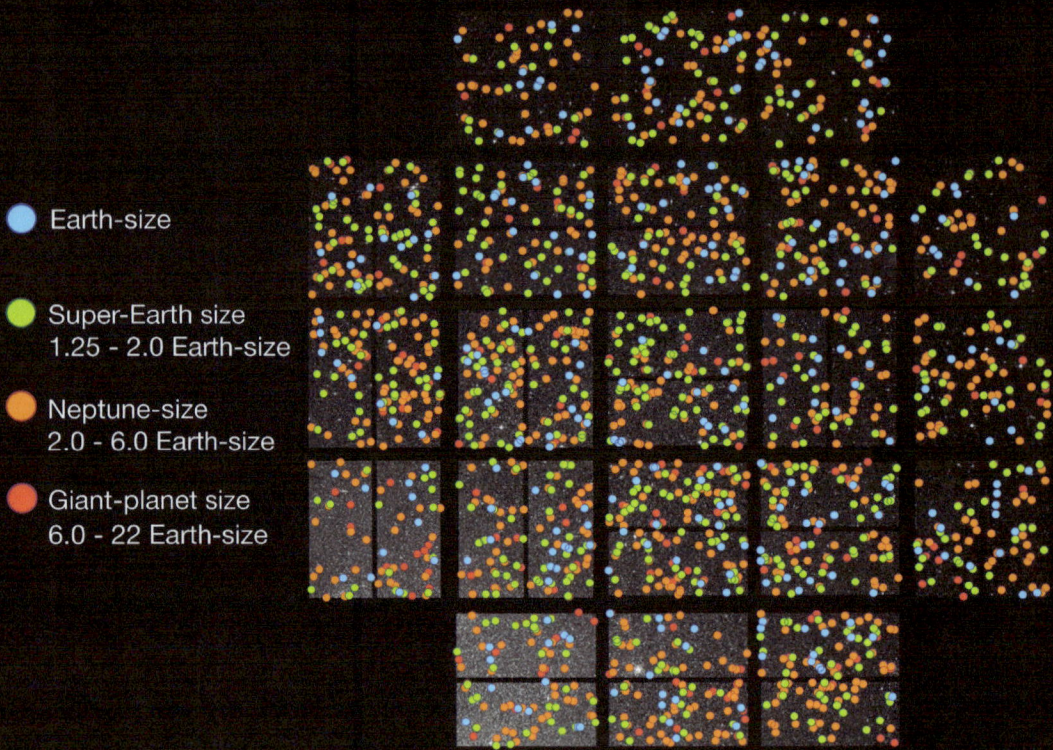

- **Earth-size**

- **Super-Earth size**
  1.25 - 2.0 Earth-size

- **Neptune-size**
  2.0 - 6.0 Earth-size

- **Giant-planet size**
  6.0 - 22 Earth-size

*Kepler has already found hundreds of planets in the small patch of sky that it studies. Some of these, shown in blue on this chart, are roughly the size of Earth.*

The Spitzer provided scientists with more information on how planets are formed. And, in 2004, the Spitzer was able to detect a very, very small trace of light. This trace of light turned out to be the beginning of a star forming. Very young stars are very far away so they need to get big enough before other space telescopes can notice them. Because the Spitzer detects heat, not light, it was able to capture images of the youngest star ever seen!

# Kepler

Launched in 2009, *Kepler* is a spacecraft with a telescope on board. *Kepler* was launched in order to search for other Earth-like planets that may exist in our galaxy.

The planets found by the Hubble and the Spitzer are very large. Their size made them much easier to see. *Kepler* is looking for planets that are about thirty times smaller than these larger planets. These "Earth-like" planets are sometimes called "Goldilocks" planets. In the fairy tale, Goldilocks tried three bowls of porridge. She does not like the first two because they are too hot and too cold. Instead, Goldilocks eats the bowl of porridge that is "just right." In the same way, scientists are looking for planets that are neither too far nor too near the sun, neither too hot nor too cold, neither too big nor too small. They are looking for planets that are "just right." Scientists do not expect to find any life on these planets. They do think that life might someday form on these planets, the same way that life on Earth formed.

In order for planets to be discovered, the *Kepler* takes pictures of a part of the sky. Scientists then search for objects in the picture that might be planets. As of June 2013, the *Kepler* had found 132 planets that scientists are *sure* are planets—and another 3,216 planets scientists think *might be* planets. Of these, only two Goldilocks planets have been found. But scientists are positive that there are more out there. Using *data* from *Kepler*, scientists are able to guess that about 17 billion Earth-sized planets may exist in our galaxy alone!

## What Are Asteroids and Comets?

Asteroids are chunks of rock that orbit our sun. Some of these are very tiny, while the largest is nearly 600 miles (1,000 km) across. If they enter the Earth's atmosphere, they burn up as meteors (falling stars).

A comet is a chunk of ice and dust that also orbits the sun. A comet, however, unlike an asteroid, has a cloud of dust and gas around it. When a comet's orbit takes it close to the Earth, this cloud looks like a shining "tail." Some comets have very large orbits, which means that hundreds, thousands, or even millions of years will pass between their appearances in Earth's night skies. Other comets have shorter orbits. They may pass near to the Earth every twenty years or so.

**Data** is information that you gather as part of an experiment.

# Find Out Even More

If you want to find out more about the Hubble telescope, going online is a great way to learn more. Suppose you want to learn about the Hubble telescope's history, or its size. Using search engines is one of the best ways to find the information you're looking for online. But remember, Google, Bing, or Yahoo can only bring you results based on the words you type into the search bar. Type the wrong words, and you won't get good results. Make sure your spelling is correct! Try searching for "Hubble telescope" using Google. Take a look at the results you get back. Here are just a few:

HubbleSite - Out of the ordinary...out of this world.
hubblesite.org

HubbleSite - Gallery
hubblesite.org/gallery

HubbleSite - The Telescope
hubblesite.org/the_telescope

Hubble Space Telescope - Wikipedia, the free encyclopedia
en.wikipedia.org/wiki/Hubble_Space_Telescope

Hubble Space Telescope | NASA
www.nasa.gov/mission_pages/hubble/main/index.html

NASA/ESA Hubble Space Telescope
www.spacetelescope.org

Google can find almost 18 million sites based on the search "Hubble telescope." But which of these results is the best for what you're looking for? Which is the least helpful to you in your search? How can you tell?

First you'll want to look at the name of each site. Then you'll want to look at the web address. Each search result also comes with a bit of information about the site. Before clicking on any result, you can learn a lot about a search result by reading these three things. After looking at just the names and addresses here, which result looks best?

At first, you might think the www.nasa.gov site looks best. That's usually a good idea, based just on the names and addresses here. The NASA site is an official site. Official sites are often the best source of information online. But visiting the sites is the next step in deciding which source is best for your search.

In fact, both hubblesite.org and www.spacetelescope.org are official sites as well. NASA runs hubblesite.org. The European Space Agency owns www.spacetelescope.org. Both sites are great resources for information about the Hubble telescope.

Wikipedia can be a good source, too. But you've always got to remember that Wikipedia isn't a perfect source. The facts on Wikipedia aren't checked by experts. The information on Wikipedia doesn't always come from a good source. You can't always be sure what you're reading is correct. Make sure to check the source for information on Wikipedia. Click the small numbers near facts that you have questions about. If there is no small number, that means there may no good source for the information. You may have to check the fact yourself to be sure it's true. Wikipedia isn't the best source on the list.

# FOUR

# What Comes Next?

As of 2013, *Kepler*, Hubble, and Chandra were still searching the sky. But all three were nearing the end of their missions. *Kepler* no longer sent back information on planets. NASA had to decide whether to keep it working, searching for other objects in space.

Meanwhile, new plans were underway for new, more advanced, space telescopes. After all, there will always more sky to search!

## Retiring the Hubble Telescope

Every piece of equipment that we send into outer space will break down eventually. The Hubble Telescope is powered by solar energy (energy that comes from the sun). Since the sun never stops shining, that's one of the reasons that the Hubble has lasted for as long as it has.

The Hubble Telescope has other parts that wear out, though. The Hubble is built of old, worn-out technology, so NASA is no longer sending

Unlike the Hubble Space Telescope, the James Webb Space Telescope will have several mirrors working together to create a single image. This lets the telescope gather much more light.

astronauts to replace parts on the Hubble. The Hubble Telescope continues to send the Earth amazing and beautiful photographs. But its parts won't last forever. No one knows how much longer it will last. By the time that you read this book, the Hubble Telescope might already have stopped sending pictures!

Many astronomers are very sad to see the Hubble Telescope go. To them, the Hubble Telescope is the greatest tool for space discovery that we have.

## Not Just Telescopes!

In addition to telescopes, many other space missions explore outer space too. NASA's Discovery Program, which launched *Kepler*, also launches much smaller, less-expensive instruments into space. These instruments are exploring our universe, sending back important data to scientists on Earth.

# The James Webb Space Telescope

Even though many people will be sad the see the Hubble go, the next great space telescope is already under construction. Planning for the James Webb Space Telescope began in 1996. Seventeen different countries are working it on. It is one of the most expensive space exploration missions ever. The total cost of the telescope will be about 8 billion dollars!

The James Webb is planned to be launched in 2018. Like the Spitzer, it will be designed to detect infrared light. The James Webb's mission has four parts:

- to search for light from the first stars and galaxies that formed in the universe.
- to study how galaxies are formed and grow.
- to understand how stars and planetary systems grow.
- to study planetary systems and the beginnings of life.

The Hubble Telescope became so well known because of the dazzling pictures it took. Unlike the Spitzer and Chandra telescopes, the Hubble takes pictures of visible light. Infrared light is not visible to the

One of the advantages that Hubble offered was the ability to swap out cameras and upgrade its equipment. However, the age of the telescope means that it is reaching the end of its usefulness.

*The Hubble Space Telescope helped prove the Big Bang Theory. By studying ancient galaxies, scientists are hoping the the JWST (shown here) will help them learn even more about the origins of the universe.*

human eye, though, so the JWST's "pictures" may not be as impressive to ordinary people. Once the JWST is launched into space, however, scientists will no doubt learn more amazing things about our universe.

Space telescopes have changed the way we view our planet, our solar system, and the universe. We will never again look at the night sky in quite the same way.

## Who Was James Webb?

James E. Webb was the second administrator of NASA. He played an important role in sending the first man to the moon.

The Hubble revealed some amazing things about our universe. Each light in this picture is a galaxy like ours—a collection of millions or billions of stars. We have only just begun to learn about what might be out there!

But some things have not changed. Like our long-ago ancestors who looked up into the night sky, we still gaze into space with wonder. The more we learn, the more we realize how amazing the universe truly is!

# Find Out Even More

A website like NASA.gov is a great source of information about the Hubble telescope and other space missions. But not every site is the same. Not every site is as good a source as NASA.gov.

And with Facebook and Twitter, remember that not everything online is a fact. And not every fact online is true. Each person sees the world a bit differently. Online, each website has its own point of view.

When you're searching for information online, ask yourself a few questions about each site you visit:

1. Who made the site? Why did they make the site? Each website is different. Think about the person who made the site and why they made it. Sometimes people make websites for reasons other than posting facts about a subject. Keep that in mind as you search for information about space telescopes and other topics.

2. Is the site you're using a good source of information? Is it a news site or official site? Is it a personal site, blog, or social media site? NASA's website is a great source of information about space exploration. A blog about NASA by an 18-year-old high school student might not be. Make sure you think about the kind of site you're visiting and the information on it.

3. Is the information you're reading on the site up-to-date? Can you find newer information on another site? An old site might not be as helpful if you're searching for the latest information about the subject.

4. How is the site organized? Can you search for topics that you want to learn more about? Is information easy to find? Are there categories you can use to find information on the site? Sometimes, the way a site is organized can have a big effect on how easy it is to use.

5. What do you like about the site? What do you think needs to be changed? Would you use the site again? Why or why not?

Picking the sites with good information instead of the sites that post bad information is up to you. But choosing between the two isn't so difficult when you ask yourself a few questions about each site. Remember that the Internet has no rules about what people can post. No one checks the facts of each website online. You've got to be the judge of which sites are useful and help you to learn more. And you have to spot the sites that aren't helpful.

# Here's What We Recommend

If you want to learn more about space telescopes and space exploration, here are some good websites and books to get you started!

## Online

Kids Astronomy: Telescopes
www.kidsastronomy.com/telescopes.htm

NASA
www.nasa.gov

Astronomy Magazine: Astronomy for Kids
www.astronomy.com/News-Observing/Astronomy%20Kids.aspx

Hubble Site
www.hubblesite.org

## In Books

*First Space Encyclopedia*. New York: DK Children, 2008.

Racine, Sheryl and Kathi Wagner. *The Everything Kids' Astronomy Book*. Avon, Mass.: Adams Media, 2008.

Scott, Elaine. *Space, Stars, and the Beginning of Time: What the Hubble Telescope Saw*. New York: Clarion Book, 2011.

Simon, Seymor. *Destination: Space*. New York: HarperCollins, 2006.

# Index

# About the Author

Christie Marlowe was raised in New York City where she lives with her husband and works as a writer, journalist, and web designer.

# Picture Credits

www.ingramcontent.com/pod-product-compliance
Lightning Source LLC
Chambersburg PA
CBHW042018080426
42735CB00002B/96